W9-BNT-592

A hilly city
with water on three sides,
a steep street
with eight curves,

cool, foggy summers
and warm winters,

people from all over the world,

sourdough bread,
fresh crab, gelato,
and dim sum,

gingerbread houses
called "painted ladies,"

cable cars, fireboats,
and pedicabs,

even abandoned ships
buried deep beneath
its buildings and streets...

What city is this?

San Francisco,
the City by the Bay.

For children everywhere — the future belongs to them.

ACKNOWLEDGMENTS

The idea of publishing *The City by the Bay* as a fundraiser was born in 1988. Since then, many individuals have contributed their time and talents to this project. Special thanks go to Tricia Brown, Elisa Kleven, San Francisco Archivist Gladys Hansen, and our editor, Victoria Rock. We would also like to thank Jill Brubaker and the rest of the staff at Chronicle Books, Laura Jane Coats, and our many community friends for their enthusiastic support. Lastly, our heartfelt thanks to those League members involved in developing, researching, writing, and promoting this book. Their vision, creativity, and dedication will be felt throughout the San Francisco Bay Area for years to come.
— *The Junior League of San Francisco*

SPECIAL THANKS
The following community friends provided invaluable assistance in the creation of this book:
Susan Faust, librarian, Katherine Delmar Burke School, San Francisco
Gladys Hansen, archivist, The Museum of the City of San Francisco
Martha Jackson, children's book buyer, A Clean Well-Lighted Place for Books, Larkspur, CA
The Japanese Consulate-Information Center Staff, San Francisco
Sharyn Larsen, owner, The Storyteller Bookstore, Lafayette, CA
The Mission Dolores Staff, San Francisco
Effie Lee Morris, board member, California Library Services, San Francisco
The Museo Italo Americano Staff, San Francisco
Rose Pak, consultant, Chinatown Chamber of Commerce, San Francisco
Neel Parikh, chief of branch libraries, San Francisco Public Library

DONATIONS FOR THIS BOOK WERE GENEROUSLY PROVIDED BY:
Bechtel Group, Inc.	Levi Strauss and Company	Pacific Gas and Electric Company
Chronicle Books	Nestlé Beverage Company	Pillsbury Madison & Sutro
Ghirardelli Square		

Copyright © 1993 The Junior League of San Francisco, Inc. All rights reserved.
Book design by Laura Jane Coats.
Printed in Hong Kong.
Library of Congress Cataloging-in-Publication Data:
Brown, Tricia.
The city by the bay: a magical journey around San Francisco
by Tricia Brown and the Junior League of San Francisco; illustrated by Elisa Kleven.
        p.   cm.
Summary: A tour guide to the landmarks and interesting sights of San Francisco.
ISBN 0-8118-0233-7
1. San Francisco (Calif.) — Juvenile literature. 2. San Francisco (Calif.) — Guidebooks — Juvenile literature.
[1. San Francisco (Calif.) — Description and travel — Guides.]
I. Kleven, Elisa, Ill. II. Junior League of San Francisco. III. Title.
F869.S357B77   1993   917.94'610453 — dc20   92-32104   CIP   AC
Distributed in Canada by Raincoast Books, 112 East Third Avenue, Vancouver, B.C. V5T 1C8
10 9 8 7 6 5 4 3 2 1
Chronicle Books, 275 Fifth Street, San Francisco, California 94103

The City by the Bay

A MAGICAL JOURNEY AROUND SAN FRANCISCO

Illustrated by **ELISA KLEVEN**   Written by **TRICIA BROWN**

and **THE JUNIOR LEAGUE OF SAN FRANCISCO**

Chronicle Books • San Francisco

For centuries, perhaps millennia, San Francisco and its Bay were known only by native peoples who lived in small communities throughout Central California. Typically, each community had its own distinct language. As a result, there was never a common name used for the population as a whole.

When the Spanish arrived, they called the natives *costeros*, or "coast people." Later, the English-speaking settlers referred to them as *Costanoans*. Today, descendants of the early natives generally call themselves *Ohlones*.

In the late 16th century, explorers from around the globe began sailing the waters surrounding the San Francisco peninsula. Since that time, San Francisco's population has been made up of an ever-changing mosaic of cultures.

How the

1579 Sir Francis Drake, an English admiral and navigator, sailed north of San Francisco into what is now Drake's Bay.

1595 Sebastian Rodrígues Cermeño, a Portuguese explorer, sailed into the same small bay, naming it *La Bahía de San Francisco* (The Bay of San Francisco).

1700's Portuguese and Spanish mariners sailed the California coast. But because of the rough shoreline, they missed the narrow entrance into a larger bay close by — that is now named San Francisco Bay.

1769 Spain founded *misiones* from *Baja California* to *Alta California*. During an expedition to find new mission sites, Don Gáspar de Portolá and his scouts accidentally discovered San Francisco Bay.

1775 Spanish Navy Lieutenant Juan Manuel de Ayala sailed the first ship through the Golden Gate Strait into San Francisco Bay — one of the largest natural harbors in the world.

1776 *Misión San Francisco de Asis* (Mission of Saint Francis of Assisi) was built. It was later called Mission Dolores after a nearby lake. A quiet pueblo called *El Paraje de Yerba Buena* (The Place of the Good Herb) grew up around the mission. The area was treeless, with rolling hills, mudflats, and sand dunes. The "good herb," which grew wild on the dunes, was mint.

City Came to Be...

1846 The crew from an American ship, the *U. S. S. Portsmouth*, took control of *El Paraje de Yerba Buena*. In 1847, the settlement was renamed "San Francisco."

1848 Gold was discovered in the Sierra Nevada foothills. In the two years that followed, San Francisco's population increased from 900 to 56,000, as the gold miners, or "49ers" (named for the year 1849) rushed to San Francisco in search of gold.

1848-1906 The Transcontinental Railway was completed, linking San Francisco to the East Coast. The railway, in combination with the Gold Rush, made San Francisco a booming city. The sand dunes were flattened to make room for buildings. Trees were planted. A seawall was built so that ships could unload their cargo onto the *embarcadero*.

1873 Cable car service began.

1906 Early on the morning of April 18th, an earthquake measuring 8.25 on the Richter scale shook the city. Streets caved in. Chimneys cracked. Buildings fell. Gas and water lines broke. More than 3,000 people died, and approximately 28,000 buildings were destroyed as a huge fire burned for three days. The west side of the city was saved by the military. They dynamited buildings on the east side of Van Ness to create a firebreak.

1914 Trolleys and buses began to roll up and down San Francisco's streets.

1927 The San Francisco Airport opened along the shore of the bay, just south of the city.

1936-1937 The Golden Gate Bridge and the San Francisco-Oakland Bay Bridge were constructed, putting an end to dependence on ferry boats, which until then had been the primary means of transportation across the bay.

1972 BART, the Bay Area Rapid Transit system, began operation, making commuting even more efficient for people coming to San Francisco from the Peninsula or the East Bay.

1989 On the evening of October 17th, a 7.1 earthquake shook San Francisco. Throughout the Bay Area, 63 people died and approximately 1,000 buildings were damaged. Again, gas and water lines broke, and fires started easily. San Francisco's water was in short supply, but a fireboat named the *Phoenix* helped by pumping bay water to portable fire hydrants.

Today Millions of tourists visit San Francisco each year to enjoy its mild climate, natural physical beauty, and diverse cultural attractions. Immigrants from all over the world continue to arrive, enriching the tapestry of city life — making San Francisco a truly magical city.

Chinatown

Gung Hay Fat Choy! That means "Happy New Year!" in Chinese. New Year's is a special time in this neighborhood, the largest Chinese community in the western hemisphere. People wish one another good luck and happiness, and children receive *lai-see* — small red envelopes filled with money.

The holiday is celebrated in January or February, depending on the cycle of the moon. Each year is named after one of the twelve animals in the Chinese zodiac. There are many parades and ceremonies. Lots of firecrackers are set off to scare away evil spirits and bring good fortune.

Chinatown is colorful all year round. Walk down Grant Avenue, with its street lights that look like lanterns and street signs written in Chinese. Look at the fresh vegetables and fruits overflowing out to the sidewalk from the grocery stores. Smell the aromas coming from all the different restaurants. Is it time for *dim sum*, a Chinese lunch?

The Japanese Tea Garden

During the month of March, the Japanese Tea Garden comes alive with the fluttering color of pink cherry blossoms. Originally designed for the California Mid-Winter Exposition in 1894, this magical five-acre garden was later embellished by master gardener Makoto Hagiwara. In the middle of the city, he created an oasis filled with the quiet of the countryside. Here visitors can cross a graceful drum bridge, have a warm cup of tea, and enjoy a fortune cookie (a treat that was invented by Hagiwara).

Amid the foliage of the garden sits a bronze statue that is ten and a half feet tall. Cast 200 years ago in Japan, it is called the *"Amazarashi-No-Hotoke,"* or the "Buddha who sits through sunny and rainy weather without shelter."

The Cable Cars and Lombard Street

Before 1922, the famous crooked block of Lombard Street was straight, and so steep that it could not be traveled by carts or wagons. The only way for people to get up and down the hill was on foot. After the invention of the automobile, the city added eight turns so that cars would be able to travel the street as well. Today, tourists wait in line to drive down this twisting street.

Visitors can also view Lombard Street from the cable car that runs along Hyde Street. Andrew Hallidie introduced the cable car to San Francisco in 1873 because he felt sorry for the horses pulling wagons up the steep hills. People laughed at his idea at first, but he didn't give up. Today, San Francisco's cable cars are a National Historic Landmark.

The Golden Gate Bridge

Looking from the Marin Headlands to San Francisco on clear evenings, you can watch the twinkling lights of the city, the Golden Gate Bridge, and the San Francisco-Oakland Bay Bridge. On other nights, when the fog rolls in, you can hear the foghorns, and feel the cool fog as it wraps around the Golden Gate Bridge like a blanket.

Although the name of this bridge is the Golden Gate, the paint used to cover it is actually "International Orange." The bridge is named after the strait at the bay's entrance — the Golden Gate.

Some people believed that a bridge could never be built across the Golden Gate, but a group of determined engineers found a way. Built in 1937, the bridge spans a length of 6,450 feet — that's longer than twenty football fields! The tallest tower is 746 feet high — as tall as a 70-story building. The amount of wire used for the main cable is enough to wrap three times around the earth.

Mission Dolores

Mission Dolores is the oldest building in San Francisco. It is one of a chain of twenty-one missions that stretch along the California coast.

Founded in 1776 by Franciscan *padres* (fathers or priests) from Spain, the original mission was a series of wooden buildings. The building you see today was begun in 1782 and completed in 1795. The walls, made of adobe bricks, are 4½ feet wide at the base. The bricks were made by Ohlone Indians, who also painted patterns on the ceiling using bright vegetable dyes. The mission's original bells, from Mexico, still ring today. You can see them in three archways beneath the tile roof.

Many of San Francisco's streets are named for historical figures whose gravestones can be found in the mission's cemetery: *Arguello, Noe, Sanchez,* and others. The Spanish influence can be found not only in the city's street names, but throughout the Mission District — in restaurants, building styles, and colorful murals.

North Beach and Coit Tower

North Beach is not a beach at all! It's the name of a colorful neighborhood filled with shops, coffee houses, and restaurants. Another name for this area is "Little Italy." That's because so many Italian immigrants made this part of San Francisco their home. It was the Italians who saved Telegraph Hill in North Beach after the 1906 earthquake: they brought out wine barrels and used red wine to douse the fire as the flames came creeping up the hill.

On top of Telegraph Hill sits Coit Tower, built in 1933. Earlier in San Francisco's history, this hill was the site of a signal station used to notify townspeople of the arrival of ships carrying mail, cargo, and passengers. Today, you can take the elevator up sixteen stories, and then climb the last thirty-seven steps for a spectacular view of the city and the bay!

The Palace of Fine Arts

Although it was originally intended as a temporary exhibit for the 1915 Panama-Pacific Exhibition, the Palace of Fine Arts was so well-loved that it was later rebuilt to become a permanent part of San Francisco's skyline. The beauty of this graceful palace is reflected in a natural lagoon, which is bordered by lawns and trees. The sight is especially stunning at night when the palace is spectacularly lighted. It's a wonderful place to take a stroll, to have a picnic, or to feed the swans and ducks.

The palace is a majestic domed rotunda, with six supporting columns, that is as tall as an eighteen-story building. The angel sculptures inside the rotunda are twenty feet tall. If you want to get an idea of how big that is, you can go into the neighboring Exploratorium and stand next to one of the original angels from the 1915 exhibition!

Union Square

One of the most famous shopping areas in the world, Union Square lights up during the holidays. A giant Christmas tree and menorah are lit, and flower stands brighten the street-corners with colorful bouquets and holiday wreaths. Department store windows come alive with storybook figures, holiday clothes, and festive decorations, as the sidewalks bustle with the crowds of visitors who come to San Francisco every year.

Union Square's name dates back to the time of the Civil War, when the northern states, called the Union, fought to prevent the south from seceding to form a separate country. Although the war took place in the east, many San Franciscans supported the Union army. In 1861, Unionist patriots led by Daniel Webster used the square as a rallying place. Ever since that time, it has been known as Union Square!

Fun Facts about the

Lighthouses, foghorns, and buoys guide ships as they navigate San Francisco Bay. Mariners identify the different foghorns by the length and frequency of their "blasts" and length of the pauses between blasts.

There are eleven islands within San Francisco's city limits: Angel Island, Yerba Buena, Alcatraz, Treasure Island, and the Farallones (a group of seven islands outside the Golden Gate).

Alcatraz — also known as "The Rock" — was the home of the Bay Area's first lighthouse. Today it is a national park, but for many years it was the site of a high-security Federal prison from which many escapes were attempted (seven of the escapees were killed, three were drowned, and five were never found).

The Bay Bridge was given a garland of 640 extra lights to celebrate its 50th birthday in 1986. A year later, 900 permanent lights were installed.

The Bay Bridge's deepest pier drops 242 feet into the water. Its tallest tower (from bedrock, below the Bay, to the very top) measures nearly 550 feet, making it taller than the largest of the Egyptian pyramids.

The Bay Bridge is actually made up of four bridges: two suspension bridges on the San Francisco side, and a cantilever bridge and a truss bridge on the Oakland side. The two pairs of bridges are connected by a tunnel through Yerba Buena Island.

In 1861, Wells Fargo Bank linked California to the east with the Pony Express. This new coast-to-coast mail service took just ten days on horseback, less than half the time it had taken before by train and stagecoach.

San Francisco Bay is not really a bay at all — it's an estuary. (A bay is filled with ocean water. An estuary is filled with a combination of salt water and fresh water.) It is the largest estuary on the west coast of the United States, and has one of the most diverse populations of marine life in the world.

Sutro Tower, San Francisco's tallest structure, transmits television and radio signals from the top of Mt. Sutro.

In 1850, when sourdough bread was delivered to San Franciscans, loaves were placed on spikes outside the doors so that animals could not reach them. Sourdough bread is unique to San Francisco — the wild yeast that is used to make it rise won't grow anywhere else!

San Francisco has more than 3,000 restaurants.

The San Francisco Ballet is the oldest ballet company in America. Founded in 1933, it was the first American ballet company to perform "Nutcracker" and "Swan Lake."

City by the Bay...

"BART" stands for Bay Area Rapid Transit, the computer-operated, electric-rail train system that connects San Francisco with the East Bay and the Peninsula.

....

BART's Transbay Tube is 3.6 miles long and rests on the Bay floor, 135 feet beneath the surface of the water. It is made up of 57 giant steel and concrete sections.

....

Chocolate was not the first product to be manufactured at Ghirardelli Square —it was originally the site of the Pioneer Woolen Mill, which produced uniforms and blankets for the Union Army during the Civil War.

Nob Hill takes its name from the Hindi word *Nabob,* meaning "one of great wealth." This was a term used to describe merchants and other people returning from Europe and the Far East with riches.

Cable cars are pulled along by underground cables that are constantly moving. A gripman pulls a lever that grips the cable through a slot in the street. When the gripman lets go, a brakeman stops the cable car with wheel and track brakes. The gripman and brakeman ring bells to tell each other when to brake (stop) or grip (go).

San Francisco's firefighters locate emergency water reserves by looking for circles on the streets. 151 intersections have large circles of bricks set into the pavement — each marks a reserve tank holding about 75,000 gallons of water.

....

During the Gold Rush, Levi Strauss made tents out of heavy denim cloth. When he noticed how easily the goldminer's pants were wearing out, he started using tent fabric to make heavy-duty pants. That was the beginning of the denim blue jeans we wear today.

....

The heaviest gold nugget found during the Gold Rush weighed 195 pounds — that's as heavy as four eight-year-old children!

Abandoned sailing ships from the Gold Rush days lie buried beneath the streets of San Francisco. The ships were covered by landfill during the city's early days of expansion.

The Transamerica Pyramid is 853 feet tall and has 48 stories — it's the tallest building in San Francisco. The Bank of America building is the second tallest — it has 52 stories, but is only 779 feet tall.

....

How do the windows of the Transamerica Pyramid get washed? They pivot open from the center so that both sides of the glass can be cleaned from the inside.

More Fun Facts...

SAN FRANCISCO STREETS

The Crookedest:
Lombard Street
(between Hyde & Leavenworth)
Vermont Street
(between 21st & 22nd Streets)

The Oldest:
Grant Avenue *(1835)*

The Longest:
Mission Street *(7.29 miles)*

The Widest:
Sloat Boulevard *(135 feet)*

The Narrowest:
De Forest Way *(4 1/2 feet)*

The Steepest:
Filbert Street
(between Hyde & Leavenworth)
22nd Street
(between Church & Vicksburg)
Duncan Street
*(between Sanchez & Noe;
not open to vehicles)*

San Francisco motto:
"Oro en Paz, Fierra en Guerra"
(Gold in Peace, Iron in War)

San Francisco flower:
Dahlia

San Francisco colors:
Black and gold

San Francisco ballad:
"I Left My Heart in San Francisco"

San Francisco song:
"San Francisco"

San Francisco patron saint:
St. Francis of Assisi

There is a dog, a cat, and a baby
in each of the large illustrations
in this book. Can you find them?

San Francisco's flag and seal
each depict a phoenix rising
from the flames — a powerful
symbol of the city's spirit.

....

San Francisco flag:

San Francisco seal:

The Bay Area has survived four
major earthquakes — in 1868,
1906, 1957, and 1989. After each
of these disasters, San Franciscans
have worked together to rebuild
their city. Just as the phoenix in
the Egyptian myth rose from the
flames, the city of San Francisco
rose from the rubble renewed.

Because San Francisco is home to people from around the world, the city's vocabulary is filled with words from many different cultures. Here is a sampling of some foreign words and phrases you might hear:

....

SPANISH

alcatraz: *(ahl-cah-tras)* pelican

alta: *(all-tah)* upper, top

baja: *(bah-ha)* lower, bottom

El Camino Real: *(ell cah-mee-no ray-all)* The Royal Highway

embarcadero: *(em-bar-cah-dare-oh)* wharf

helado: *(eh-lah-doh)* ice cream

misión: *(mee-see-yone)* settlement with church

península: *(peh-neen-soo-lah)* almost an island

presidio: *(preh-see-dee-oh)* fortress

pueblo: *(pweh-blow)* village or town

taquería: *(tah-kay-ree-ah)* taco shop

ITALIAN

focaccia: *(fo-cah-chee-ah)* chewy Italian bread seasoned with olive oil and herbs

gelato: *(jeh-lah-toh)* ice cream

pasticceria: *(pah-stih-cher-ee-ah)* Italian pastry or pastry shop

trattoria: *(trah-tor-ee-ah)* restaurant

....

CHINESE

Dai Fow: *(die-ee fah-oo)* Big City*

dim sum: *(dim sahm)* heart's delight, pastries

Du Pont Gai: *(doo pont guy)* Grant Avenue

gai: *(guy)* street or avenue

Gum Lung: *(gum lung)* Golden Dragon, a mythical beast used on festive occasions as a symbol to ward off evil spirits

Gum San: *(gum sahn)* Golden Mountain*

Both names refer to San Francisco.

Gung Hay Fat Choy: *(gong hay fah choy)* a greeting used during the Chinese New Year; it means "Wishing you become prosperous."

Sun Neen: *(sun-neen)* Chinese New Year

....

JAPANESE

cha-no-yu: *(cha-no-yoo)* tea ceremony

hondo: *(hohn-doh)* worship hall

Nihonmachi: *(nee-hon-mah-chee)* Japantown or a Japanese neighborhood

sushi: *(soo-shee)* vinegared rice rolled in seaweed, in a small ball or in a bowl; topped with foods such as raw fish and cucumber, and garnished with ginger and horseradish

udon: *(oo-don)* noodles

The Explorer's Guide

Ride BART, a cable car, pedicab, taxi, trolley, boat, bicycle, bus, or car to visit these attractions!

ON THE BAY
Take a ferry to **Alcatraz Island** for a tour of the old Federal prison, or to **Angel Island State Park** for a day of hiking and picnicking.
Ferry information: 546-2805

IN CHINATOWN
Watch fortune cookies being made at the **Golden Gate Fortune Cookie Company**.
56 Ross Alley; 781-3956

The **Chinese Culture Center** offers free changing exhibitions and Heritage Walks through Chinatown, as well as special programs during the Chinese New Year.
750 Kearny Street; 986-1822

NEAR THE JAPANESE TEA GARDEN
Surrounding the Japanese Tea Garden is **Golden Gate Park**, with over 1,000 acres of trees, plants, lakes, and meadows. A few of the highlights are:

M. H. de Young Museum
863-3330

Asian Art Museum
668-8921

Strybing Arboretum and Botanical Gardens
661-1316

Golden Gate Park Carrousel
666-7201

The California Academy of Sciences, which includes:
Morrison Planetarium
650-7141

Steinhart Aquarium
221-5100

Natural History Museum
750-7145

ON THE CABLE CARS
Ride either of the Powell Street cable car lines to the **Cable Car Museum** to find out how cable cars work.
1201 Mason Street; 474-1887

NEAR THE GOLDEN GATE
Become a "cannoneer" at the cannon drills at the **Fort Point National Historic Site**, tucked under the south end of the Golden Gate Bridge.
556-1693

See military artifacts from the Spanish settlement through the Vietnam War at the **Presidio Army Museum**.
Funston Street & Lincoln Avenue, Building Two; 561-4115

Across the Golden Gate at the **Bay Area Discovery Museum** you can build a "high-rise," fish from a ship "on the bay," take a hike with a naturalist, and more.
332-7674

INSIDE THE PALACE OF FINE ARTS
Twist a tornado, play in the Shadow Box, or make your own fog at the **Exploratorium**, a hands-on science museum.
360 Lyon Street; 561-0360

NEAR UNION SQUARE
Originally modeled with children's dough, then cast in bronze, the **Bread Dough Fountain** by sculptor Ruth Azawa is a wonderful view of the City in miniature!
Next to the Grand Hyatt, 345 Stockton Street

JAPANTOWN
Drink tea in a tatami room at one of the many restaurants in **Japantown**. See the Peace Pagoda, shops, and dance and martial arts demonstrations at the **Japan Center**.
Bounded by Post, Sutter, Laguna and Fillmore Streets

AT THE CIVIC CENTER

Attend a performance of the ballet or the opera at the **War Memorial Opera House**.

301 Van Ness Avenue; 621-6600
San Francisco Ballet; 703-9400
San Francisco Opera; 864-3330

....

In **Davies Symphony Hall**, enjoy a performance by the **San Francisco Symphony**.

201 Van Ness Avenue; 431-5400

....

At the **San Francisco Museum of Modern Art**, see the collection of paintings, sculpture, and photography.

401 Van Ness Avenue; 252-4177

ALONG THE WATER

Take a hike at **Land's End** for a panoramic view of the Golden Gate Bridge, the Marin Headlands, and the Farallon Islands.

Learn about off-shore wildlife at the **Visitors' Center**, located on the lower level of the **Cliff House**. Nearby, you can play coin-operated games at **Musée Mécanique**, or walk inside the giant **Camera Obscura**.

All at the Cliff House; 1090 Point Lobos Avenue; 387-5847
GGNRA Visitors' Center; 556-8642
Musée Mécanique; 386-1170
Camera Obscura; 750-0415

....

At **Fort Mason Center**, enjoy art exhibits and educational programs provided by a variety of organizations:

African-American Historical and Cultural Society
441-0640

Mexican Museum
441-0404

Museo Italo Americano
673-2200

Young Performers Theatre
346-5550

All at Fort Mason Center, Marina Boulevard and Buchanan Street

See chocolate being made at the **Ghirardelli Chocolate Shop and Soda Fountain** in Ghirardelli Square.

771-4903

....

Explore historic ships at the **Hyde Street Pier** and visit the exhibits at the **San Francisco Maritime Museum**.

556-3002

For a look at San Francisco history, visit the **Museum of the City of San Francisco** in the Cannery. Special attractions include an exhibit on the Great Earthquake and Fire of 1906.

2801 Leavenworth; 928-0289

....

OTHER PLACES OF INTEREST

At the **Basic Brown Bear Factory and Store**, you can take a tour and stuff your own teddy bear or mouse.

444 DeHaro Street; 626-0781

The **Randall Museum** is a children's science museum, offering many classes for pre-schoolers to adults.

199 Museum Way; 554-9600

....

See performances by and for children throughout the year at the **San Francisco Children's Opera**.

245 10th Avenue; 386-9622

....

Operating hours of all attractions can vary according to the season, so call ahead for hours and details of current features (all numbers listed are within the 415 area code), and remember to dress in layers. San Francisco's weather changes throughout the day.

Enjoy the City by the Bay!